The Worst Book I'll Ever Write

The Worst Book I'll Ever Write

How to overcome perfection and publish your first book in just five days

Antoinette Johnson

Copyrighted Material

Copyright © 2012 Antoinette Johnson
All rights reserved.

ISBN-13: 978 - 1475124781

Antoinette Johnson

*To Mum, Nathaniel, Grannie Roses and Grandad
I've done it. I've written and published my first book*

The Worst Book I'll Ever Write

Contents

Acknowledgments	9
Preface	11
Introduction	13
Do You Know Why You're Writing?	19
Back to this Perfection Thing	23
The Essence	27
The Worst Book I'll Ever Write	31
Writing The Worst Book You'll Ever Write	35
The Four Steps	39
The Bonus Step	51
Summary	53
The Proof is in the Pudding	57
I Love The Worst Book I'll Ever Write	61

The Worst Book I'll Ever Write

Acknowledgements

God, thank you for your Word and thank you for the title and idea for this book.

Jennifer Beaumont-Whyte, after speaking to you about so many book ideas I've finally written and published one. About time too huh?

Uncle Tim, thank you for the space I needed to dedicate five days to writing and publishing my first book.

The Worst Book I'll Ever Write

Preface

I'm a perfectionist. I've wanted to publish a book for years. I've had more book ideas than I've had hot dinners. I've started writing more books than I can even remember. I'm tired of being that person who's always *writing* a book. I want to be that person who's *published* the book.

Sod it! Even if it turns out to be the worst book I'll ever write, at least I can say I've written and finished one, no?

I had twelve ideas for books I wanted to write. Some were How-to types, others were stories and although the ideas were in my head, I thought about all the research I needed to do, I thought about how I'd have to develop the story, I scanned the internet looking for information that would help and I literally felt the fear of turning one of these ideas in to a writing mess; What would people think? What if I couldn't communicate my story well enough?

I went to bed that night feeling frustrated and began to wonder if I really was cut out to write. I'd written stories since I was a child and was writing on my blog at **www.annyonline.com** , I'd even written a poem (and I'm no poet) that I thought was pretty good, but somehow being unable to transform the ideas in my head into published books led me to begin questioning whether I would ever be good enough to create a proper book that could be published.

As I dosed off to sleep that night, the title of this book came to me; 'Write the worst book I'll ever write, how to overcome perfection and publish your first book in five days'. I woke up the next morning with this still on my mind. It sounded like a crazy idea but I really liked the idea of taking away any pressure to be good, to write well, to research or develop a book well and was excited by the thought of actually finishing something in five days. I decided to put all the other ideas to one side and give it a go.

I followed my steps and you're reading the result - proof that it works!

I'm a published author of The Worst Book I'll Ever Write. What a great title!

Antoinette Johnson

Introduction

Are you fed up of starting 'A Book'? Are you having so many ideas for books that you're driving yourself crazy? Have you been searching online, reading writers' blogs and watching YouTube videos hoping to come across that one Top Ten Tip, that one piece of advice, that one analysis of successful writers, that will give you the secret to getting that manuscript (blah...even the word seems like a chore!) finished? Are you struggling to get your idea from your head to the paper and wondering if you really are cut out to be a writer? Do you dream about being a bestselling author and being approached by that American movie company that wants to turn your story in to a box office hit?

If this is you, then I empathise and encourage you to keep reading as I hope the content of this book will help.

Publishing a book in the 21st Century is easy so there's no practical reason why you shouldn't be publishing your ideas and stories. In today's technologically advanced world, you no longer need the approval of a publisher to get your work to the Market. In fact, with all the online ways that you can communicate and interact with people these days, it's so easy to connect with your Market directly. I read an article online today about a guy who has sold over one million copies of his eBook by self-publishing, so you really do have the power.

There appears to be a problem though because many of us aren't publishing and I believe getting our ideas out of our heads and on to paper is the biggest problem. If we could only get those words on paper and uploaded to a self-publishing site, we'd make huge headway in the world of writing and in our businesses wouldn't we (I know some of you want to write a book to put your business on the map). So I guess we can agree that the blockage exists in the writing stage, yes? Even when we get the ideas and start writing, we get stuck don't we? Some of us can talk about our idea until the cows come home, we know what we want to include and may even voice record ourselves hoping to use that to help us transfer our thoughts to paper, but when we sit in front of that piece of paper or computer screen, the flow freezes like the fresh water in Churchill, Canada (Just a place I heard about recently and thought I'd throw in – look it up when you've got a mo!)

May I make a suggestion?

Perfection is getting in your way.

We've grown up in a society that encourages us to get things right, the fear of getting things wrong and being rejected often causes us to try our best to please and get things as right as humanly possible. Whether that means staying up all night to get a project completed or not showing others our work until it's 'finished'.

The reality, whether we like to admit it or not, is that even when we believe that we've completed something to perfection, or to the best of our ability at least, we're still growing, developing and learning so it will always only be as good as the point that we're at when we finish it. Have you ever looked back on a piece of work you completed a few years ago - work that you thought was fantastic - and cringed at it? The essence may still be there but the way you put it together just isn't as fantastic as you thought back then, is it?

This is the reason why waiting for perfection is a waste of time – you'll always measure the standard of something relative to yourself. It will be measured against what you know and what you've experienced. If your knowledge and experience is always growing and expanding, your standard will continue to change. This means that if it takes you a year to write a book, the standard you used to measure it when you first started, will be totally different to what you measure it against a year later. Therefore if you're chasing perfection, you'll be chasing a moving standard and your book will never get published.

Maybe you're afraid of putting out substandard work. Maybe you worry about it affecting your reputation or people laughing at it. Let me put those fears to bed; Writing the worst book you'll ever write is about you – if you don't want to share it with anyone else, then don't, no one is forcing you to. I just want to help you get those creative juices flowing and get moving with your writing ambitions.

The intention of this book is to help you get over the 'perfectionitis' that's preventing you from publishing that first book of yours. Yes, I just made up that word and Word is highlighting it to me with a red line, but I'm afraid it's staying as it is.

At the moment your desire to create the perfect book is overpowering your desire to publish a book. Hopefully by the time you finish reading The Worst Book I'll Ever Write, you'll start rethinking this hierarchy of desire and follow the steps to getting your book published.

I don't want you spending hours and days reading this because it's really a very simple process and if I was attempting to write the Best book I'll ever write, I may try to offer lots of commentary and extras to fill out the book (and overcomplicate things) but we know that I'm not trying to do that and I'd rather you start taking steps towards becoming a published author than reading about it, so I haven't made this book too long. The length is also another example of my refusal to exercise perfection, most books need thousands and thousands of words and I'm guilty of having typed the 'How many words should my book have' question in to Google. I'm sure one day I'll get there, but right now, I'm writing for three days and that's it, whatever the word count is. Some of you may even appreciate that.

Antoinette Johnson

Do You Know Why You're Writing?

I know there are some writers who write because they simply have to write. I'm not one of them. I've been told that the best way to determine what you are most passionate about is to find that thing that would send you crazy if you couldn't do it. I'm quite sure that if I couldn't write, I'd remain sane; tell me I could never travel by air again and then you'd have a loopy loo on your hands. So, I've admitted to myself that I don't write because I love the process of writing but write because I have a desire to see my ideas given their own identities, whether that's in books or in movies and I aspire to have a bestselling book, a story turned in to a movie and to do a book signing with people who love and connect with my work – a girl can dream. I actually enjoy the process of thinking about the idea and the storyline in my head more than writing it down.

I'm sure I'm not alone in this and it's probably why there are so many aspiring writers who are trying to convince themselves that they enjoy writing, when actually they'd give anything to just hold that book with their name on it, tightly in their hands without having to write a single word. Is that you?

Many of the literary agents, publishers and even successful authors that have posted videos on YouTube to help us write great content and get a publishing deal, say that not many publishers will accept your first piece of work. Only last night I watched a guy who said that if you have more than one book, it shows a commitment to writing. I came to the conclusion therefore that there really is no point spending hours and days and weeks and months and years ploughing my way through one idea when the chances of it being accepted are slim. I could turn out to be the next JK Rowling and have all of that invested time remarkably rewarded but as someone who will find it very challenging to stick with one story for 17 years without seeing any fruits of that labour, I doubt that will be my path.

Instead it makes more sense to get that first book out of the way. Call it the foundation. Call it the point from which you will improve and use to build up to that bestseller you really want. This is what this book will help you to do; get that first book done and out of the way.

The Worst Book I'll Ever Write

Antoinette Johnson

Back to this Perfection Thing

Perfection is a journey and not necessarily a destination. It's a journey of continued improvement. We all want to improve at whatever it is we do. The sportsperson trains to improve, the artist draws to improve and writers write to improve, whether that's building stamina, discovering new colours or developing a writing style, they want to improve. In everything in life, we always aim for better, no? As writing is a constant journey of progression and improvement why spend so much time on the first step – that first book. Why not get the ball rolling, get something out and then build from there.

While you're agonising over creating one perfect book (I use the word perfect very loosely here), you could have written five books, each getting better than the other, released five different ideas that you have locked up inside you and made greater overall improvement.

Can I also let you know that you're probably much better at writing than you think you are? It's highly likely that when it flows naturally, it comes out a lot better than you realise. It's when you put pressure on yourself, trying to conform to the way it *should* be done and what others have done, that you move yourself from the unique space you own into a tight box that is not conducive to expressing the ideas that *you* have.

Sometimes the mind has a bit too much control, telling you what you can and can't, should or shouldn't do. In order to fully engage in the process of creating this book, you'll have to get that little voice in your head under control. You can try to cover its mouth, but as with most people you try to gag, they try even harder to speak, so this may not be a very successful method and will just be a waste of energy.

My advice is simple. Sit down quietly and explain to your mind that this project, this book, is about creating the worst book you'll ever write. You are purposely creating something that you expect to be full of mistakes, flaws and errors.

Also remember that once you publish this book, the expectation is that people won't like it; how could they possibly like the worst book you're ever going to produce? When they point out why it's a useless and awful attempt at writing, be happy and keep your focus on why you wrote it; you wanted to create a foundation on which to build and where better to start than at the bottom.

The Worst Book I'll Ever Write

Antoinette Johnson

The Essence

If you have a desire to write something, there is obviously something that you feel the need to share with others. I call this The Essence of your book. Whether it's something you know and want to share with others in a How-to book or a storyline you think will be interesting to explore and potentially entertaining for others, you have something inside you that you want to share and communicate with other people. If you don't do this, you are losing out on expressing part of you and the world is losing out on experiencing that part of you.

People are waiting for the essence, give it to them

Words can create fluff or substance around your essence. In most good/great books, those words are usually substance, but I have to say that as someone who often reads with a highlighter pen, I usually end up highlighting sentences here and there that stand out for me and form the message that I get from the book. I'm also guilty of skipping pages in novels when descriptions and scene setting gets too long, drawn out and intense. A shame, as I'm sure the authors invest a lot of time creating these parts. This is not to say that words of substance do not help to get a message across to the reader, but it's something we can look at when we have a first book to build on, right? For now, we're interested in finding the essence and communicating that in its rawest form. People read books because they want to be entertained or they want to find out something; does it matter if we keep them reading for a week, a month or just an hour?

In this imperfect book, we just want to share The Essence and get moving. We're not thinking about the word count we use to do it, setting scenes or structuring things so as to share it in the easiest way; we've got one thing in mind – we want to get the essence out there. You can make them wait for years until you've polished it or you can give it to them now just as it is.

If people don't like the way you've written then that's cool, you got the essence of that idea out and your writing can improve next time, after all, this wasn't meant to be a good book was it.

You are waiting to express your essence, indulge yourself

Not only are others waiting for your essence, you are waiting to express your essence too. Don't spend a minute longer holding in what you MUST share with the world. Don't go through frustration and boredom waiting to express it. Let it go and see how great you feel.

When you write what excites you, that'll be the best place to be. If you're bored at having to write a certain part of the book, what makes you think the reader won't get bored too? It's just my theory and belief but I think it makes sense that if you're enjoying what you're writing, that will ooze through your words and cause someone else to enjoy what you're writing too.

When your book is finished, release it without expectation, without fear and without perfection; Just get it out there and start the next one.

Antoinette Johnson

The Worst Book I'll Ever Write

Hopefully by now you're getting the idea and reason behind writing the worst book you'll ever write as a way of overcoming perfection. Here are some thoughts that might help you stay focused and actually enjoy the process.

Writing the worst book you'll ever write means...

.....that your book doesn't have to be good, great or even OK.

.....that you don't expect any success from it

.....that you're doing this just for you

.....that you don't need to be good at writing or possess any talent or skill in this area

You're free. Just get exactly what you have in your head, into a book, in whatever way it comes out.

During the process of writing The Worst Book I'll Ever Write, I thought about what I believed *Good* books should be. Can you relate to any of these beliefs?

A Good book is the product of months of invested time

To write a good book an author has to spend many hours locked away from the world, writing, rewriting, developing characters and losing themselves in the world of their good book. Only when they come up for air, with the polished version, can they happily share it with the world and wow us all.

A Good Book must be a certain thickness

For a book to be a Good book it must look like a book and not a booklet, right? We don't pay for booklets do we? It must be thick enough to convince us that there's enough value for us to exchange our hard earned cash for it.

A Good book must flow

By flowing we expect the good book to keep us moving through it in an orderly fashion. It must grip us at points when we expect to be gripped, it must trigger emotion and connection that causes us to stay attached to the story or message and we must feel the value of all that time the author invested in writing and structuring it for us.

A Good book is written 'well'

Good books are written by people who have a way with the English language aren't they; those exceptionally skilled people who know how to weave words and grammar together to create a masterpiece. When it's written well we gladly give the author the credit that they deserve.

The beliefs I held about Good books gave me some insight in to what my book was going to be; I wasn't going to spend long writing it, it wasn't going to be thick, it wouldn't flow or engage the reader and it wasn't going to be written well. I would give myself just five days to take it from idea to a finished document, it would be as long as it needed to be in order to put my points down in five days, I would write according to the plan and write as if I was speaking through the book; if that meant failing on engagement, flow or writing well, then so be it.

Writing The Worst Book You'll Ever Write

I'll share how in 4 steps you can finally get those thoughts from your head and in to a published book but there's one small bit of preparation that you need to do first.

I've mentioned that I gave myself five days to complete this book and before I share the four steps that made this happen, I'm going to instruct you to spend five days doing this too. I don't mean five evenings or five mornings, I mean five dedicated days. If it means taking time off work, sending the children to stay with family or you locking yourself in a room by yourself, do it! This is the launch pad for your writing career and if it's not important enough for you to find five days to dedicate to it, then maybe you should ask yourself if you really want to publish a book, hey that could be the reason why you haven't published anything already. Besides, if you can't find five days, what makes you think that you'll find the year to complete that 'perfect' book?

I know life is full of responsibilities, distractions and unexpected events, but I'm just being honest with you here when I say, if you start spreading your five days over a month or two months, you'll get bored, frustrated and you'll have so much time to think about the idea, the writing and the story that you won't produce your best 'worst' work and you'll miss the whole point of this process.

At the end of the five days, if you've followed these steps, you will have the worst book you'll ever write (the launch pad for creating better and better work) uploaded to a self-publishing site and at the printers ready to be admired by its creator; You. So go on, sort it out.

The Worst Book I'll Ever Write

The Four Steps

Now you've set aside your 5 days all you need to do is follow these four steps:

STEP ONE

Think of an Idea
(Day One)

STEP TWO

Plan the Outline
(Day One)

STEP THREE

Write it
(Day Two – Day Four)

STEP FOUR

Self-Publish
(Day Five)

Ok, Ok, so these steps are nothing new, right? This is the process you've spent the last _____ (fill in the blank) years*/months*/weeks* (circle as appropriate), trying to get through to get that idea from your head to the world, yes? I hear you, but please stick with me here. I'm not so much saying that there's an easy way around this process, what I'm suggesting is that there's an easier way *through* the process that many of us have struggled with.

It requires a shift in thinking, from perfection to imperfection and a focus on getting that first book published and in your hand rather than trying to create a bestseller that the world will love. This shift gives you the freedom you need for your creative juices to flow. There's no forcing or squeezing taking place. It compresses the process in to a short time period so you'll stay engaged, enthusiastic and get the result you want; a result that will kick start your writing career.

Think of an idea

Think of an idea. I'm sure if you've thought about writing a book, you have at least one idea you could use for this project and one idea is all you need. Don't think about it for too long, remember it doesn't have to be the perfect idea, with the perfect storyline, perfect instruction or even the perfect character. It just needs to be an idea that you'll be happy thinking about for five days. Don't analyse the idea, worry about whether people want, need or will love the idea or if you have the writing skill to do the idea justice. Just take one idea and go for it and once you've decided, stick with it.

I know you may have an idea that you don't want to use for the worst book you'll ever write, it's too good an idea for that, right? Well here's the thing - use it! What's stopping you going back to your finished, published book and creating a newer edition? Get the idea and let's go!

Plan the outline

The next step is to brainstorm the idea and turn that in to a plan of what you're going to write. Apparently it's not acceptable to use the word brainstorming anymore, but as this is an imperfect book, I'm using it. Empty your essence through brainstorming, bullet points, lists, anything that gets it out, but don't use a computer; get your pen and paper out and start scribbling.

Now plan how your scribbling will be put in to your book – what order will each part appear in your book and what do you want to say where. This is the step that provides the bones of the story or the information that you're going to share through your book. What points, diagrams, examples, people and places are you going to include, if any? Remember to keep it simple, don't overcomplicate, over think or make it more of a chore than it should be. It shouldn't take you more than one day to complete and it doesn't have to be a concrete, neatly presented plan with clear chapters, it just needs to be your essence organised in such a way that you'll be able to write when you reach step three. You may come back to this step at various points during the writing stage so don't worry if you forget something.

Write it

This is the bit you have a love/hate relationship with isn't it? It's the part that makes you a writer, yet it's the part that has stopped you turning in to a published author. It's that mountain you've attempted to climb on numerous occasions and found yourself heaped at the bottom time after time after time. It's the journey that you've never got to the end of and been able to sit and say 'That's finished'. It's the part that successful, published authors tell you is "hard work and not as easy as you aspiring writers with your rose-tinted glasses on, think it is" (can you hear the resentment in their voices? Only joking, we love and admire all you successful writers really!).
Well, relax, we're approaching things differently, you are going to write, but you are going to keep it

short, sharp and sweet. Don't think about writing thousands of words or expanding on those things you think should be expanded but seem to be too boring or take too long. The point of this step is just to keep your idea in mind, follow your plan and write it down.

Just write. Don't think about the style, flow, dialogue, words or grammar. Just write.

At this point you could use the computer as its quicker, and remember, the most important thing is that you *just write*. This is not the time to think too much about what or how you're writing; it's the time for you to use your fingers to let your essence flow. Write as it comes and do as little re-reading as possible (I know this is a habit you'll have to fight!). If you start getting bored with a part of the story, end that part immediately and move on to another bit. Remember, if you're bored, the chances are the person reading will be getting bored too!

Keep writing for three days only (I mean it!) and when you reach the end of the third day, read through it once, correcting any obvious spelling or grammatical errors and making any obvious changes. Try to ignore the urge you will inevitably feel to restructure or rewrite too much of it. This is just a final check to make sure there are no glaring mistakes that you can quickly and easily fix. After this final check, leave it as it is. After all, the goal is to create an imperfect book, a book that will be the worst book you'll ever write, right? If you start changing too much, you'll be on your way to missing the five day deadline and back to the realms of a book that will never be perfect enough for you to release in to the world.

You may find that you've written everything in your plan before reaching the third day. That's fine, rather than go over what you've already written, brainstorm some more. See if there're any other relevant bits of information, parts of the story, descriptions, examples or anything that would add to the content. Don't add stuff for the sake of it, but make sure you have poured your whole essence in to this book, not fluff, but the core essence of your message or your story.

If you know what your title is, a trick I found helpful was to write the title and the subtitle on a piece of paper and get in to a zone of writing down everything that comes to mind when you think of it. You may come up with ideas that arose during your first planning session, but there may be additional things that you hadn't thought of before.

If you are still stuck for more to write and the three days is not up, this is the point at which I give you permission to read your work from beginning to end. Make sure you have your note paper and a pen to hand and make a note of any additional thoughts that are sparked by the content you've already written. When you've read all the way through, go back to your notes and write them in.

If you really cannot think of anything else to write that isn't fluff, then stop. The worst book you'll ever write is finished. Yaaaay!

If you're still writing from your plan at the end of day three and have more to write, I'll give you a one day extension but at the end of that extra day, you MUST stop! The Worst book you'll ever write is finished. Yaaaay!

The hardest part is over. Take a deep breath and smile.

Self-Publish

This is the last day of the process. You've written and have the document that will turn in to your finished book. Before you get in to the self-publishing process I want you to do one thing first. Find a quiet space and read through your writing one last time, but read it out loud as if you were reading it to someone. This may sound like a very strange thing to say but **please read your words**! It's amazing how often we read something out loud and include words that aren't even there – trust me, I've done it myself. If you said a word and it's not in your document, add it now! If you've stumbled as you've been reading, then reword that part so that you can read it fluidly.

When you've done this, it's time to move on to the publishing bit.

When I got to this step I was amazed (read as *overwhelmed*) by all the things I had to think about when it came to self-publishing and the different options available. I did underestimate the 'upload to a self-publishing website' process and found myself caught up in reading the blogs, the articles and the *a* vs *b* self-publishing forum discussions, trying to decide which one to use. Which one prints the best cover? Which royalty option should I choose? Which distribution channel should I opt for? Should I pay for editing and formatting support? But fortunately for you I did all of that and came to a simple conclusion; it doesn't matter!

It doesn't matter if the cover is great quality or not, you don't need to pay for a professional to edit your work, it doesn't even really matter which distribution channel you choose. Why? Well because you just want a copy for you and if it sells, that's great you'll deal with that bridge when and if you come to it. Don't stress or think too much about that now, you'll slow yourself down.

The other thing that I was alerted to during my online surfing, were these eBooks; they're taking off you know and from the little I saw, it's even easier to publish an eBook than it is to publish a book, so why not see your book in all available formats, it's free!

I decided to use Amazon's self-publishing arm, CreateSpace for print and Kindle Direct Publishing for the eBook. The decision was based on simple common sense (well common sense in my mind anyway); I use Amazon and know of the Kindle and I know they're known and used quite a lot by other people. Simple.

No deep and meaningful reasons, just based on my limited experience and knowledge of this world of technology. Even if it turns out to be the wrong choice, I'm sure I can address it at a later date, why worry about it now.

At CreateSpace, Lulu.com and other self-publishing sites, you upload your document* and create a cover, it doesn't have to be anything special, all you want to see is your title and your name on the cover. Get a proof sent to you and sit with a treat (could be a glass of wine, a box of chocolates or some other indulgence), holding your book in your hands, smiling and finally being able to say "It's finished, I'm a published author".

*CreateSpace provide blank templates, so to save time copying and pasting at the self-publishing step, I'd recommend using one right from the start and write in it. The self-publishing company you use may have their own templates available, so check.

Any marketing or promotion of your published work is entirely up to you. Maybe you'd like to just have the book available on your blog/website or utilise some of the free/paid for distribution options available online but whatever you choose, remember that the goal was to get your mitts on a copy of the worst book you'll ever write regardless of the response to it, so by completing this process you're already a success, well done!

If your book becomes a sudden hit and you gather a loyal following you may attract traditional publishers to your work and why wouldn't they take on a book with a large following that you've invested your time, energy and belief in building, hey, you've done much of the hard work for them. However, please stay focused and remember that Self-Publishing in this process is more about getting that copy of your first book in your hands and your essence out in to the world than it is about publishing to sell and wow people, therefore don't be disappointed if the publishing companies don't come running.

With this piece of raw work, you're more likely to come across people who will point out the flaws, errors and mistakes you've made and if they do, that's great, after all this is a piece of imperfect work that you've created. Self- Publishing gives you the freedom to get your hands on that book and make your imperfect book available to the masses even if they don't want to buy it.

Warning!!

Just when you think the writing is over, you discover that when you start the process of self-publishing, you have to write a description for your book – aaaaarrrrghhhh!! I know, I know, more writing. Don't panic. Always stick to the 'this is the worst book that I'll ever write' theme, therefore just write whatever you believe best describes your book and don't worry about how it reads, the style or the length (there is a limit but you've got plenty to work with).

Antoinette Johnson

The Bonus Step

Before you race off and start this process, there's a bonus step that I'd like to share with you. It's the key step in the process of getting to that bestseller and that movie deal!

BONUS STEP

Repeat

Just keep repeating the first four steps, aiming to improve with each book. By the time you create that bestseller you'll have a whole back catalogue of books that your readers will be able to search for, read and enjoy and you'll be buzzing with excitement at seeing the fruits of the ideas that were once locked away inside you. Your collection of books will also show publishers that you are a committed writer with lots of ideas. You no longer need to try and convince them through lots of chat, you'll have evidence that you may not be the greatest writer yet, but you have the ability to get those ideas out of your head and in to books, that alone will put you a step ahead of the rest.

Antoinette Johnson

Summary

To help you out a little I thought I'd put together a short summary.

You have an essence that people are waiting for and that you need to express.

Waiting for perfection will not help you experience growth and improvement as a writer or get closer to that bestselling book.

How to get over perfection...

Focus on what you want; a book published in your hand, a finished product, getting those thoughts and ideas out of your head.

Make imperfection your perfection in this project

The goal is imperfection; to have a finished imperfect publication of your thoughts and idea in your hands with your name on the cover.

Don't worry about what people will think, your project isn't perfect so if they find flaws, mistakes and errors, that tells you that your project is a success. The only way is up from there.

Realise that what's perfect to you right now, won't be perfect this time next year because you grow, learn and change with time.

...and publish something

The Process

1. Think of an idea
2. Plan the outline/bones of the idea
3. Write it
4. Self-publish

Bonus Step: Repeat

When you have that finished book in your hands;

You can say you're a published author

You set the foundation on which to grow as a writer and author

You know you can start *and* finish a book

The Worst Book I'll Ever Write

The Proof is in the Pudding

If you're sceptical about whether you can really publish your first book in five days, the proof is staring you right in the face. This is the process that I went through to be able to express my essence and publish my first book and if I can do it then you can too.

Step One: Think of an idea

The idea to write The Worst Book I'll Ever Write about writing the worst book I'll ever write came to me and I could see myself focusing on it for a short period of time.

Step Two: Plan the outline

After lots of brainstorming I identified 6 key areas that I wanted to cover. These became the first titles I worked with before brainstorming some more during the 'Write it' step and adding more content.

Step Three: Write it

I got in to the idea so much that I wrote more than 3000 words in the first four hours. I continued to write, adding bits that came to mind and referring to my plan that I'd done. You know you're on to something when your body wants to go to bed but your mind is begging it to stay awake so that you can write some more. What you see in here is the result of *just writing*.

Step Four: Self-publish

As I said, this step was quite overwhelming and not as easy as I initially thought it would be. I spent much of my allocated time trying to decide which company to use and copy/pasting my text in to the template. Once I got my mind back to what I was doing; writing the worst book I'll ever write and realised that many of these decisions didn't matter, I was flying through the process.

If you have this book in your hand or are reading it on an electronic device, you can be assured that I'm smiling and patting myself (gently) on the back, at having published my essence in a book that will be the worst book I'll ever write. Now I've done this, it's onwards and upwards for me!

The Worst Book I'll Ever Write

I Love The Worst Book I'll Ever Write

Who would've thought I'd finish a book called The Worst Book I'll Ever Write and love it so much. I said you should try to ignore the urge to reread your work, but I have to admit that I keep rereading and rereading, not changing and restructuring but admiring the fact that having spent years trying to write and finish a book, I've actually done it. I never expected that I'd feel so proud of something that will be the worst book I'll ever write.

It's tempting to continue writing and thinking of 'fluff' to add, especially as it hasn't taken me three days to write, but I know I've expressed as much of The Essence of this idea in this book as I can and anymore will spoil it.

No it's not tens of thousands words long, it may be tricky for you to follow in parts and the writing style may not get me nominated for any literary awards, but who cares – I love it!

It symbolises a project that I started *and* finished, it's the first time I've been able to get my message out in to the world through a book and I've proven the strong message I've shared in the book and strongly believe in – *The desire to do things perfectly is a hindrance to getting stuff done so get over perfection and do something today, I did!*

I now feel like getting started straight away on all the other ideas I've had whizzing around in my head for years. I just want to get them out, even if I build up a collection for me and me alone, it feels great to release this stuff and I really do feel lighter already. If others like what I write and share then that'll be good, but having gone through this process and come out the other side, I realise that that's not actually the most important thing after all.

Printed in Great Britain
by Amazon